Signs and Wonders from Our Journals

Signs and Wonders from Our Journals

by Carole Duncan Buckman

Saint Mary's Press
Christian Brothers Publications
Winona, Minnesota

This book is lovingly dedicated to Mother and Dad.

Genuine recycled paper with 10% post-consumer waste.
Printed with soy-based ink.

The publishing team included Carl Koch, series editor; Stephanie Weller Hanson, development editor; Laurie A. Berg, copy editor; Gary J. Boisvert, designer, production editor, and typesetter; Maurine R. Twait, art director; pre-press, printing, and binding by the graphics division of Saint Mary's Press.

Printed in the United States of America

Printing: 9 8 7 6 5 4 3 2 1
Year: 2006 05 04 03 02 01 00 99 98

ISBN 0-88489-532-7

Contents

Good morning, Lord. It's the first day of school,
and I'm sitting in the assembly.
New clothes, new haircut, blank notebooks—
it's the all new Michael.

We have a new principal, a man.
Kids say he'll be really tough.
He has steely gray eyes, and he's tall.
What did his smile mean when we came in?

It's starting now. We pledge allegiance under God.
The new teachers are being introduced one by one.
I hope they like me, Lord.
I hope they haven't already formed opinions,
because it's a new year,
and I'm going to study this time.
Do they really save those behavior slips
piling up in my file year to year?

Help me, Lord, to do my best.
Walk beside me today,

and help me keep my mouth shut
and my mind on learning.

Thanks, Lord, for Miss Swensen.
She is so beautiful, and she liked how we sang.
Her hands flew over the piano,
and we sang funny songs with hand motions
just like we did in the primary grades.

I'm sorry I threw Juan's lunch out the bathroom
    window.
It happened so quickly.
I just got caught up.
I haven't met with the principal, Brother Edward,
    yet.
He was really busy with the first day and all.
Jesus, I know it's a lot to ask,
but could You make him forget
that he wants to see me?
He has a lot to do, after all,
and I'm only one sorry, skinny kid,
easy to forget.

Well, Lord, I've been polishing windows.
I suppose it was too much to ask
that Brother forget me.
He wasn't so bad, really.
He didn't yell or anything,
and he said I'd have a clean slate
after I washed the windows
and brought Juan lunch for a week.

I left Jenny a note in her spelling book.
I told her how pretty she is
and that I am glad she's in our class.
I disguised my handwriting
and didn't sign my name.
Lord, You know the future.
Will Jenny ever think I'm special?

Gotta go. The bell is ringing.
Stay with me today.

Jesus, we signed up for flag football.
All the guys in the seventh grade signed up,
so we'll have a great team,
except none of us is very big.
And Ben, the quarterback, isn't doing his
    schoolwork,
so he might be ineligible by the first game.
If he is, Lord, could You put in a good word
for me with the new coach?
I've been practicing passing to my sister,
and she thinks I'm pretty good.

I suppose You noticed my A in spelling.
Thanks for all Your help.

Jenny knocked my books off my desk
and giggled with Susan and Frances.
Does that mean she likes me
or that she thinks I'm a dork?

Brother Edward said hello to me by name again.
He sure has a good memory.

Football practice starts this
    afternoon.
I can't wait.
The guys in class haven't
    done any work today.
Mrs. Garza passed out
    novels.
She expects us to read fifty
    pages a day.
Isn't that an awful lot?
Can't You tell her that we have
math and science and football?

Jesus, I should just stop going in that bathroom.
I never meant to throw water on anybody.
Ben started it. And You know my temper.
I guess it wasn't temper.
I might have been mad for a minute,
but then it was just fun.
Bubba looked so funny all wet like that.
Brother Edward says I'll have detention all next
    week.
I'll miss the first thirty minutes of practice.
Coach said I could come on over after that.
Thanks for keeping him on my side at least.

Boy, was I wrong about Miss Swensen.
She's a witch. She made me write one hundred
    times

that I would not throw anything over the balcony.
She kept us waiting outside the class
for a long time while she flirted
with the coach in the gym,
and I only sailed two paper airplanes
over the balcony.
I suppose You saw them?
It must be neat that You can send out
a bunch of birds flying everywhere
without some grouchy teacher interfering.

We had Mass today. Did You like how I read?
It was cool standing up there in front.
I felt powerful, like somebody.
Didn't You think my voice carried well
over the microphone?
I suppose You planned it all—
part of my rehabilitation.
You did give me an advantage
by making Brother Edward always think of me,
so I was the one chosen to read.
Do You have big plans for my voice?
Could I maybe announce football games?
Or how about MTV?
It'd be fun to be there with all that music and stuff.

Jesus, can't You tell them I'm innocent?
I know You were falsely accused and all,
but You weren't a kid then.
It's hard to be like You.
We don't know what happened

when You were growing up in Bethlehem.
Maybe there were kids who got You in trouble
with Mary and Joseph and folks at the temple,
so You know how I feel.
I think it was Juan who put the smoke bomb
in my locker.
The note on my desk was printed
that told me to leave math class
and go to the bathroom,
just when it filled the hall.
You know who did it.
I hope You punish him good.
Could You please give Mom some
    comfort,
some sign that I'm not a criminal?
She took my suspension awfully hard.

Here I am, Jesus, with Mrs. Perkins,
because neither Dad nor Mom could stay home
    today.
She won't let me watch TV.
I finished my schoolwork this morning.
Now I've got nothing to do
except read Mrs. Garza's novel.
We're supposed to have it finished tomorrow.
Did You make all this happen
just to get me to catch up on that boring book?
I mean, who cares about Indians anyway?
I guess You do. I guess You care about everyone.
I'll read it.
I hope You're keeping track
of all these good things I'm doing.

Jenny didn't talk to me this morning.
She's such a goody-goody.
I was only suspended for one day.
You'd think I was dealing drugs or something.

We'll get our football uniforms this afternoon.
Coach put his arm around me
and said he hoped I'd keep my nose clean.
That's a dumb thing to say,
especially because I have all these allergies,
and I really do have to keep a pile of tissues with
     me.

Why did You let Miss Swensen move me to the
     back?
I was not making faces. She imagined it.
I left Jenny a note in her spelling book.
I suppose You didn't like it that I said she was
     getting zits.

Well, I've stayed out of the bathroom,
but it hasn't helped.
I was not running with the television and VCR
     cart.
Hurrying maybe.
Why would Mrs. Garza send me anyway?
They all know I'm not responsible,
and they keep putting me in spots where I get in
     trouble.
Thanks for Your help on the novel test.
Mrs. Garza probably thinks I cheated.
Tell her I deserved that 100.

Don't I look cool in my football uniform?
Mom took my picture.
I tried to look fierce,
and she kept saying, "Smile."
My sister says I'm going to star in the game.
Thanks for my sister.

Juan admitted he set the smoke bomb.
"No hard feelings," he said.
I shook his hand.
I know You say to forgive
    others as You forgive
        us.
I hope You've noticed I'm
    trying.
Jenny said she'd dance
    with me at the first dance
        on Friday.
The girls all had cards to fill out,
like they used to have a hundred years ago.
Susan read about it in some book.
I have to dance with Louise, too,
because she was standing there looking at me,
and I couldn't hurt her feelings.
She's really fat, You know.
Maybe You could help her with that.
She does have a nice smile.

Seven stitches. Were You watching, Jesus?
Mr. Freeman said we weren't supposed
to hang from that basketball hoop,

but no one ever said what would happen if we did.
I guess I probably saved someone else, right, Lord?
Everybody will be careful from now on.
Someone else won't bleed because I did.
That's like You offering Yourself for us, isn't it?
Brother Edward drove me to the emergency room.
He said he was surprised to spend so much time
    with one kid.
I didn't know what to answer.
Lord, I started all new not many days ago.
I'm truly sorry I've messed up.
I know when I say that, You'll let me start over,
and You'll forget about all the bad stuff.
I wish You'd remind Brother Edward
about forgiveness and clean slates.

Well, the science teacher called in all of us who sit
    in my desk.
Someone's been carving again.
I think it was the fourth grader with the shifty eyes
who kept stuttering.
It sure wasn't that little Katy.
I've never seen anybody so shy.
She needs Your help, Lord.
We're a bunch of sharks around here,
and she'll never survive.
I said I'd stay after school tomorrow and sand it.
I'll have to protect my stitches.
I told the teacher it wasn't an admission of guilt,
but that, because no one was admitting it, I'd
    repair it.
She, of course, KNOWS I did it.
Put it on my record, Lord.

I'm innocent.
It might have been done by the public school kids
who have religion classes at night.
They're always doing stuff.

I talked to Katy in the hall afterward.
She's a sixth grader, and they can come to the
    dance.
I said I'd like to sign her dance card,
and she said she didn't have one,
but I told her I'd dance with her anyway
if she wasn't dancing with someone else.
You need to give her some courage, Jesus.
You did okay with the looks.

My hand itches like crazy.
I sanded the desk.
Brother Edward came by to look
    at it.
I told him my theory about the
    public school kids.
He smiled at me, I think.

I'm all ready for the dance.
Thanks for talking Mom into the loafers.
I knew I couldn't do it alone.

Jesus, that dance was great!
Thanks for how everything worked out.
They still haven't found out
who kicked a hole in the wall in the boys' bathroom.
At least they know I didn't do it.

I was dancing with Louise at the time,
and all the kids were laughing,
so everybody remembered.
When I realized they were laughing,
I kept her dancing, and for someone so fat,
she's really light on her feet.
I don't know why You let people laugh at other
    people.
Maybe You meant that I was supposed to do
    something about it,
and that was why I stayed with her.
Anyway, thanks for how it turned out.
They all know I'm an innocent man.

Katy was there for a little while.
I got her some punch,
but she wouldn't dance.
Jenny giggled and watched other people
the whole time we danced.
She's awfully concerned about who's watching her.

Miss Swensen announced that we're having a play.
I put my name on the top of the list for tryouts.

My hand is looking a lot better.
The doctor says I can play in the first football
    game.

I hope You've noticed my grades.
All that homework is paying off.
I suppose I owe it all to You.
First You gave me the brains,
and then You helped me really do the work.
Anyway, thanks.

Jesus, how could You let it happen?
I've worked hard. I've hardly had any trouble.
Now the teachers are all filling out papers about me.
They want to test me for being hyper.
Tell them I'm normal.
I don't want to take medicine all the time,
like glassy-eyed Norman.
Norman used to be such fun.
Now he trudges around with his head down.
I know I sharpen pencils a lot.
I can't stand a dull pencil,
and I have to get up out of my desk to sharpen
    them.
You know my nose runs.
I can only make so big a mountain of tissues
before I have to walk to the wastebasket.
I know I don't keep my feet still.
If they're still, my fingers are tapping.
It's the way You made me.
Surely it can't bother anybody
    too much.
I think it all started with that
    smoke bomb.
I can't tell them that Juan did it
because I shook his hand.
I have a doctor's appointment on Monday.
They want me to be a zombie.
Help me, Jesus.

We won! Thanks, Jesus, for handing me the ball.
Thanks for tripping the kid from Saint Louis.

It was so great.
Jenny kept calling my name,
and she looked so cute in her cheerleader uniform.
Dad was proud of me,
and the pizza victory party was perfect.
I'm sorry I complain all the time.
You have given me many blessings.

Everybody thinks I'm a hero.
It almost keeps me from thinking
about my appointment after school.
Jenny left me a note in my spelling book.
She wants my phone number.

Poor Louise. I think she's getting bigger.
It was her birthday,
and we sang "Happy Birthday," but all off-key.
It was embarrassing.
Jesus, why do You let us be so cruel?
I hope You liked the poem
I left her on her math book.
"Roses are red,
Violets are blue.
I hope this birthday
Is great for you."
I didn't sign it,
but I wanted her to get one nice thing.

Jesus, that doctor was nuts.
There are certain things a kid expects of a doctor,
and this guy wasn't normal.
What was I supposed to think

when he threw the wastebasket
right after I came into the room?
It hit the wall.
And those questions, where did they come from?
If there's anyone who needs medicine to get through
    the day,
I think it's that doctor.
He kept asking me if I thought everyone was out to
    get me,
like everybody was plotting.
All I said was that I didn't like
teachers filling out forms about me.
Please help him write his report.
I missed practice because of the appointment.
It's raining now, so today's is canceled.
Thanks for the rain, though. It smells so good.

Jesus, when Miss Swensen called me in,
I thought I was in trouble again.
Thanks for persuading her to take a chance on me.
I know that she's nervous about giving me the part.
You heard me promise her I'd learn every line
and do my best. You know I meant it.
I can't wait for the show,
especially because I'm a star.
Help me to follow through on
    my promises.
Thanks for the flier about
    altar servers.
You must have left it on the steps for
    me.
When I was a fourth grader,
my parents didn't have time to drive me to the
    church,

but now I can get there myself on my bicycle.
I've always wanted to be an altar boy.
I left the form at the rectory after school,
because they must have picked up the others
    already.

Thanks, Jesus, for the good altar-server practice.
I don't care if I'm the only seventh-grade boy.
It's going to be fun.
Why is Brother calling me in tomorrow?
The note said 8:00.
I don't think I've done anything.

Please help Sis pass her driving test.
She's a little worried.

Dad's hearing rumors about his company going
    bankrupt.
Please keep an eye on things there, too.

Well, I never touched the ball, did I?
But I did stop a touchdown,
so it wasn't a total loss.
I would like more playing time, Lord,
and the team would like to win.
I know You're listening to the other guys pray, too,
and we all want to win.
I trust You to sort it all out fairly.

I'm not sure what happened with Brother Edward.
He waved my application at me and asked,
"What's the meaning of this?"
I told him I wanted to be an altar server.

"The class is for fourth graders," he said.
"How did you even get an application?"
I told him how I'd always wanted to serve Mass,
and that I figured You'd left the form for me.
He put the form down and sighed.
"You're serious?"
I said I was.
"You're not going to disrupt the class of fourth
    graders?"
"No, sir," I said.
And then he waved me to the door.
People can be servers into high school,
so why does anyone care if I start late?

Louise cried in class today
after no one chose her to be in their project groups.
How can You watch that stuff and not do
    something?
Or maybe You were doing something
when You had me notice.
Ben and Bubba agreed she could work with us
if she and I do the work.

I'm getting a kick out of Katy's little sister in the
    play.
She steals the show.

Thanks for helping Sis.

Thank You for the nutty doctor.
I'm normal. Thanks for the ice
    cream Mom treated me to.

I'll try his strategies.
Mom and I bought a
    bunch of pencils
so I'll have a supply
    sharpened.
Thanks for the new novel.
I love mysteries.

Jesus, I know You have everything under control,
but Dad is awfully worried.
I won't be able to stay at Saint Ignatius
if he loses his job.
It'll be off to public school for me.
I could get into a lot of trouble there.
I hope You're remembering that.

Thanks for the rain, again.
Everything looks better washed clean.
The football field will be perfect tomorrow.

Thanks for having me work with Louise.
She has really good ideas,
and she does her share of the work.
I hope You're thinking about reducing her size.

Jenny just called to wish me luck in the game.
She giggled a lot. I think she likes me.

Lord, I can hear Mom and Dad arguing.
They never used to do that.
Please help all of us through this tough time.

Jesus, it's late, I know,
but then You don't sleep, do You?
Thanks for my touchdown.
But I would have traded a hundred touchdowns
if You'd kept Dad in his job.
The church teaches that You turn all things to
    good,
and I hope You plan to do it fast.
Dad loved his car.
Taking it back to the dealer tomorrow will really
    hurt.

Thanks, Jesus, for all A's on my report card.
I never thought I'd do it.
Brother Edward stopped me in the hall and shook
    my hand.
Thanks for the swell job Louise did typing the report.

I'm sorry I left candy wrappers under Juan's desk.
If he hadn't talked his way out of it, I would have
    owned up.
I know how it feels to be falsely accused,
but I did enjoy his sweating.

Jesus, it was fun to have the class with those fourth
    graders.
They think I'm great.
Everybody needs to be admired, I guess.
We'll start serving Mass next week.

I'm getting butterflies about the play.
Don't forget about Dad.

Jesus, I know You're watching
    Ben cheat.
He cheats on every test.
It's not fair, is it, that I study,
and he gets the same grade?
I'm sorry I laughed
when he copied the wrong page for social studies
and missed every one.
Why didn't Mr. Freeman notice that?

The guys say I should slack off,
that everybody would be better off
if I didn't get 100s because things would be scaled.
It's hard to know, Lord.
I want to be part of the gang,
and yet I know You expect me to make the most
of what You've given me.
I keep thinking, too, that I may have to leave,
and I'd better use my time well
before I get sent to public school.

Dress rehearsal tomorrow.
Miss Swensen found me a top hat.

First Mass today. Jesus, I felt so close to You.
Thanks for letting me begin with an eighth grader.
Mary made it easy. It's nice to see girls on the altar.

I thought about telling Brother Edward about Ben.
He was there watching football practice,

and Ben was showing off.
It doesn't seem fair.

They canceled our cable TV today.
Please help Dad find work.

Jesus, humility is supposed to be good,
but I've had enough.
I wouldn't have tripped if the guys hadn't laughed
when I came out at dress rehearsal.
The show seemed pretty good though,
and everybody clapped a lot. Thanks for that.
Please don't let me mess up tomorrow night for the
    real show.

Jesus, about Toby, that fourth grader with the
    shifty eyes,
he's a real mess.
Where have You been with him?
When I found him in the stairwell
tearing pages out of the encyclopedia,
I couldn't believe it.
I got him back to class,
and I returned the encyclopedia
and all the torn pages,
but now the librarian doesn't trust me.
Like I told Brother,
the kid is already smashed like a bug—
telling on him can only hurt him more.

Thanks for helping me through the show.
Sis and the folks said I was great.

25

I really had fun.
Katy's little sister was super.

Jesus, I know life isn't supposed to be easy
and You have to balance everybody's needs and
    requests,
but how did itching powder in my football jersey
fit into the plan?
Juan did it, I know, but all the
    guys were in on it.
Everybody was laughing and
    watching.
It was embarrassing. I thought
    they were my friends.

Thanks for the minute with
    Toby at lunch.
He said his day was better. Everybody
    doesn't hate him.

Jesus, why did You let it happen?
You gave me the opportunity.
Everything was hanging there.
I was early to get ready for Mass,
and I couldn't resist.
I put on Father Murphy's chasuble and stole
to see how I'd look in the mirror,
and there was Father, glaring at me,
yelling so people could hear him way out in the
    church.
You could have kept him away for two more minutes.
Brother says I'll never serve Mass for Father Murphy
    again.
He says I'm lucky I didn't get expelled.
I told him I didn't mean any harm,

that I only wanted to see what I'd look like.
So they're blessed garments.
I'm a blessed kid, aren't I?
I really liked serving Mass
the only time I did it.

Jesus, I keep thinking about Father Murphy.
He sure has a temper for a priest.
Shouldn't he be more understanding so he can
    help people?
All the kids heard about me being thrown off the
    server list.
Louise said she was sorry.
Jenny ignored me all day.
The guys thought it was neat and crazy
that I dressed up like the priest.
You know I didn't do it to be crazy or bad.
I just wanted to see myself.

Lord, about Dad. He didn't get dressed today.
Or shave. And I think he's been drinking.
Our family needs Your help.

Thanks, Jesus, for old Father Coupal.
I've never seen him around before.
I guess he's just here visiting.
I found him in the garden behind the rectory,
talking to the plants.
His scowl didn't scare me
once I heard him talking to the lettuce.

He said I could serve his Mass
if I'm at the chapel by five minutes to six in the
    morning.
Brother said I couldn't serve for Father Murphy.
He didn't mention anyone else.
I'm going to bed right now.

It was tough to get up,
but when I rode out in the dark on my bike,
it was glorious—cold, fresh, wonderful.
There were three old people
    kneeling in the dark chapel,
and Father Coupal was in the
    sacristy getting dressed.
Lighting the candles was neat.
And he gave me bells to ring. I love
    the bells.
Why doesn't Father Murphy ring bells
    for the Consecration?
I didn't mess up, even when he went into Latin.
I didn't laugh when he stood up for the homily
and said, "Love God's trees."
I'll bet I've heard a million homilies,
and that's the only one I remember.
Maybe I got thrown off the server list so I could do
    this.

Lord, the Halloween party is tomorrow,
and Jenny is going with Ben.
I was tempted to drop one of her notes
on Mr. Freeman's desk today,

but I just kept passing them on to Ben.
Passing notes is bad, right?
But not betraying is good, right?

Mass this morning was awesome.
With Father Coupal it's so alive.
You never know what he's going to do.
"Care for God's children," he said.
I tried to think of something I could do for Toby.
I finally sat with him at lunch
and listened to him complain
about how the kids pick on him.
I hope You count that as caring.

Jesus, I realize that I shouldn't tease Mr. Freeman,
but he doesn't know Quentin Z. Wing didn't exist.
He has us doing reports on Texas history.
When I asked him if I could report on Quentin Z.
    Wing,
he said, "Sure." I couldn't resist.
I've used real events in real places,
just like they did in *Forrest Gump,* You know.
Everybody thought it was all right to put him into
    history.
You'd stop me, right, if I shouldn't do it?
Rewriting history is so much fun. Only Louise
    knows.

Mom says it's nice that I'm going to Mass every
    morning.
We need the extra prayers, she says.

Party tonight. Wish I had a new shirt.
I turned in the Quentin Z. Wing paper.
There's no going back now.
I didn't get Father's sermon today,
"Circles within circles."
I've been thinking about it.

Jesus, have You forgotten me?
Dad slugged me. My eye is going to be black.
He's never hit me. And then he cried.
That was worse. I shouldn't have said,
"You'll never find a job lying around here."
It's true, though. He can't just give up.
We're depending on him.
How could he cry? Like he
    couldn't help it.
He's always told me to be a man.
I know he didn't mean to hurt me.
I thought that when you grew up,
you didn't do things you didn't
    mean to do.

The party was okay.
Thanks for Katy dancing with me.
I thought Jenny's outfit looked cheap, didn't You?

My eye is gross, purple and green.
Father Coupal noticed it.
"You're a good boy," he said.
It made me want to cry, somehow.

"Watch sparrows," was his message today.
When I came home for breakfast, Dad was gone.
Mom is carpooling so he can have the car.
Maybe what happened yesterday was good
if it made him get up and do something.
Sis quit her drill team.
She'll have more time to baby-sit or get some other
    job.
It was expensive, but she loved it.
Jesus, give her lots of points.

What's wrong with Juan?
He walked right into the door of history class
    today.
When Dad slugged me,
I told people I'd walked into a door, I know.
But this was real. It happened right in front of me,
and he was confused afterward.
I asked him if he was okay, and he said, "Huh?"
He even walked past his desk like he didn't see it.
His eyes weren't right, either.
It was like he was sleepwalking.
I told Mr. Freeman that Juan was acting funny,
but he waved me off and went back to his sports
    magazine.

"Taste and smell and listen."
Father's words were easy today.
We had a school Mass.
I have no idea what Father Murphy said.
He needs to listen to Father Coupal.

Dad didn't get work again.
Mom was throwing up this morning.

Juan was absent today.
I was right that something was wrong with him.

Our last football game is tomorrow.
Thanks for the A honor roll.
I love report cards this year.
Jesus, I'm a little worried that Mr. Freeman
has hung up my Quentin Z. Wing report in the hall.

Mom is working too hard.
She has circles under her eyes.
Please keep Dad looking for work.

Thank You, Jesus, for Brother Edward.
He says he'll pay my tuition until my folks can do
     it.
After all the trouble I've been,
you wouldn't think he'd do that.
He says that the second grading period convinced
     him
that I'm a kid they need at Saint Ignatius.
I hope I can live up to his expectations.

Why did I invent Quentin Z. Wing?

Juan's in the hospital.
I know I've asked You to send
     him the plague and stuff,
but now please help him.
Mr. Freeman says he has cancer.

Father Coupal paused for about five minutes this
    morning in Mass.
He's getting awfully old. Please help him, too.
"Get your accounts in order," he said.

Mr. Freeman says we can't visit Juan.
He can't be around any people with germs.
He's had an operation and will have chemotherapy.
Jesus, make him well.

Mom was more cheerful this morning.
Thanks for Sis's job at the drugstore.
Father Coupal is sure moving slowly.
"God gives." Thanks for Your gifts.

The girls are leaving Louise out again,
and she looks so sad. Are You watching?

Jesus, thanks for taking my paper off the wall.
It was making me nervous there.
Somebody who knows history might read it.

"God takes away."
Father's words keep bringing up Juan for me.
You won't really take him away.
He's going to get well.
We all signed a big card for him.
The hospital is clear across the city,
too far to visit him even when he can have visitors.
The guys are talking about shaving their heads
so we'll look like Juan when he comes back.
It sounds like a cool idea.

Miss Swensen is casting the Christmas play,
and You know I'd like to be in it.
But I was thinking that now that football season is
　　　over,
maybe I could get some work after school around
　　　the neighborhood.
Can You help me with that, please?

Mom's going to the doctor tomorrow.
We don't have insurance anymore, so she must
　　　really feel bad.
Take care of us, Jesus. Remember Juan.

I'm in trouble now! Quentin Z. Wing.
Brother grew up in Massachusetts.
He doesn't know Texas history,
and he's entered my paper in the Young Historian's
　　　competition.
When he told me, I was so shocked I didn't say
　　　anything.
I had the secretary make me an appointment for
　　　tomorrow at 8:00.
I'm going to need help there, Lord.
Heavy-duty help.

"On eagle's wings." I've tried to
　　　soar today, Lord.
It may be my last at Saint Ig.
Mom's driving in now. I've got to
　　　hear the doctor's report.

34

I know You create all life, but this is not a good
time.
Mom and Dad can't have a baby now,
but I guess it's going to happen.

Thanks for the way Brother listened.
I told him that my historical research was valid,
and that I wove Quentin Z. Wing into real history.
He flipped open his rolodex without saying
anything,
and then called a Mr. Draper
and asked that my paper be withdrawn.
"Do we have a pattern here, Michael?" he asked.
When I asked him what he meant, he said,
"The tricks you pull end up making me look bad."
I told him that he'd never look bad for helping out
a kid.
Juan's going to get to come back to school in two
weeks.
Thanks, Lord.

I knew something was wrong
because the old people were standing outside the
church.
Mr. Henning said that Father Coupal
had been taken to the hospital during the night.
Thank You, Lord, for those old folks
who cared enough to wait to tell me this morning.
Please watch over Father.
I know he's had a long life and his time is about up,

but serving his Mass every morning has meant so
    much to me.
Could You give him some more time to be with me?

I can't understand the change in Dad.
Everything should be worse with the baby coming
    and all,
but he's whistling and smiling and repairing
    things,
just like his old self.
It's a miracle. Thanks.

Mrs. Wright says I can take the twins to the park
and play ball with them
every afternoon after school for two dollars.
It's not much, but I took it.
I guess it was the best You could do for
    a twelve-year-old.

Jesus, they won't let me in to see Father Coupal.
It was easy to ride my bike over to that little
    hospital,
but they have him where there aren't any visitors.
I'd really like to see him, if You could arrange it.

Mr. Freeman hasn't said anything about my paper.
I guess Brother didn't tell him. Thanks.

I talked to Toby about his problems today.
It's hard to talk about God. I mean, it shouldn't
    be—
I talk to You all the time—
but to outsiders it sounds fakey.
Anyway, the kid sure needs Your help.
He has trouble with his parents, with his teachers,

and with the other kids.
All he has is trouble.
So I showed him this
prayer journal.
I know it's between us,
but I thought he might
try talking to You
if he saw how it works
for me.

He picked right up on that entry where I called
him shifty-eyed.
"That was before I knew you," I said, and he
calmed down.
Sorry I wrote that. I never meant to hurt him.
Anyway, he said he did carve the desk.
He read my journal for a long time,
and then he said he'd try writing.

Jesus, I hope this is a good idea.
I noticed a kid walking around
at the hospital in a robe,
so I thought, in the morning when I'd usually go
to Mass,
I'd put on my robe
and see if I can't get into Father Coupal's hospital
room.
I'm going to need some guidance here.

Thanks for Dad's job.
Selling paint isn't what he wants to do,
but it's a job.

I cut out a newspaper story
about a City Rec Center exercise class.
It's for fat people, and they also talk about nutrition.
I gave it to Louise. Now she's mad at me.
Lord, tell her it's for her own good.

Jenny called me. She says that she's tired of Ben.
She wants me to help her with her math tomorrow.

Those twins are a pain. They whine and fight.
Is that what we seem like to You,
complaining all the time?

When Father Coupal woke up and grabbed my
    hand,
I knew I'd done the right thing.
It wasn't hard to slip in through the emergency
    entrance
and put on my robe in the restroom.
I think You were helping me there.
He told me about all the babies he's baptized
and all the confessions he's heard.
He sounds like me keeping track of my good
    points.

I apologized to Louise,
even though I didn't do anything wrong.
I talked to her a long time.
She's afraid to go to the class.
She's afraid that it won't make any difference.
Jesus, I'm sure You heard, but I've agreed to go
    with her.
I'll race from the twins to the Rec Center,
and then be late for dinner every night.

What's more, the twin money is going to pay my
    fees.
You're directing all this, right?

Thanks for my family. We
    seem to be happier with
       less and less.
Mom's stopped throwing up.

I thought I'd had it when the nurse
    came in.
You must have helped her understand
    about me and Father Coupal.
She said I can come without the bathrobe
and even wrote me a note for the emergency room
    guard.
"Father Coupal asked for 'The Boy' all day," she
    said.
He's never called me anything but Boy.
I guess he has too many things in his old head to
    ask my name.
He was counting prayers today.
You must have listened to millions of his prayers.
He moved his fingers along his rosary with one
    hand
while he held on to me with the other
and talked in his crazy way.
Jesus, I know You have a special place prepared for
    him.

Louise and I begin class this evening. I need major
    help there.

Well, You took him to heaven.
It was sad to find the hospital bed empty.
I asked in the office, and they said he'd be buried
    in Florida.
You'd think they'd have a Mass here, too.

The twins are catching better, still whining.
Miss Swensen said she was disappointed in me
for not trying out for the play.
She said that she'd worked hard with me
and she expected more from me.
Do I owe her something, Lord?
You know why I didn't try out.
It really made me mad. I know, I know.

Thanks for getting me into that exercise class.
I didn't think they were going to let me stay.
I liked my line about
discriminating against the weight-challenged.
Did You put that in my head?
Anyway, the class wasn't bad.
Staying in the back row was a good idea.
There sure are a lot of fat people.
Wasn't Louise's mother surprised when she met me?
I guess she thought I'd be large, too.

Well, thanks for bringing Juan back to us.
We'll do all we can to help him.
We took turns carrying his books.
Being sick hasn't changed him.
He still wants to throw paper wads and be one of
    the guys.

He wants to pull a tremendous prank. He's thinking.
He hasn't lost his hair yet, but he's so thin.
He can hardly pick up his books.

I've been trying to come up with two words,
like Father Coupal's sermons,
to think about for the day. Great God.

I stopped to explain to Miss Swensen
that I needed to work and that was why I wasn't
    trying out.
She kissed my cheek.
    I couldn't believe it.
Thanks, Jesus, for keeping
    the hall empty.

I helped Jenny with
    math during lunch.
What she wants is for
    me to give her the
    answers.
I know that's not good for her,
but it's sure easier than making her
    understand.
All she wants to do is play around.
I'll try to do better next time.

Class again with Louise. The others have accepted
    me.
Thanks, Lord, for fitting me in.
Louise has promised to cut out one piece of toast
and one dessert and her afternoon snack.
She thinks she can do that. Help her, please.
We start weigh-ins next week.

World hunger.
I see all those fat people,
and I think of all the hungry people,
all those African children.
Why do You let it happen, Jesus?
You're with me all the time. You care.
So are You with those children?
I guess I turn to You the most when I'm in trouble,
so maybe You're more with them in their starvation.
I really don't understand, Lord.

Thank You, Jesus, for Dad's promotion.
Because he's in the office now, we'll have insurance.

Juan wants to make a water-balloon catapult
that will soak the after-school bus pickup line.
I promised to work on it. His hair is almost gone.
We'll all meet Saturday for haircuts at the mall.

Brother wants me at 8:00 in the morning.
He can't know about the water balloons.
Jesus, I know I'm going to get in trouble
for the water balloons.
But Juan needs it, and I'm ready to take the fall for
    him.

Toby showed me his prayer journal.
He has been writing. He's really trying,
and I haven't found him in trouble lately,
so maybe journal writing is helping him.
Please reach out to the little guy.

Thanks, Jesus, for the rosary from Father Coupal.
It's funny that they've been looking for me ever
    since he died.
He left it to "The Boy."
The old people from Mass didn't know my name
and neither did the nurse.
Brother kind of shook me when he said,
"I thought we said you couldn't serve Mass
    anymore."
I explained that he'd said I couldn't serve Father
    Murphy's Mass.
"But you were serving Mass again?"
"Father Coupal needed
    me," I said.
"When I heard that a
    boy had sneaked into
       the hospital,
I had a pretty good idea who
    it was," he said.
I was really pleased when he gave
    me Father's rosary.

Well, Jesus, it's been a nice Christmas.
Thanks for being with us.
Thanks for the idea of giving baby stuff to
    everyone.
When he gets here, the little guy will be well
    equipped.
I really appreciated it that Father Murphy called
and said I could serve one of the Christmas Masses.

"I'll give you one chance," he said.
I know Brother must have talked to him.
Thanks for not letting me mess it up.

I've been drawing catapults.
I think if we climb out the window over the outside
    porch,
we can soak the pickup line with water balloons
    and escape
before anyone figures out where they came from.

Juan's dad practically carried him
up to Communion on Christmas Eve.
A chill went down my back when I saw that.
Shouldn't he be getting stronger?
He's so thin. His clothes look too big.
Surely he'll be better by track season.
He loves running. We won't win anything without
    him.
But we'll have him, won't we?
The twins loved those kites, didn't they?
They're not such bad kids.
Taking care of them paid for my Christmas
    presents.

Jenny called. She wanted me to meet her at the ice
    skating rink.
Jesus, it's hard to be a kid without any money.
She didn't understand.
She said she was going to see what Ben was doing.
I need some help accepting.
God gives. Father Coupal said that once.

Juan sounds awfully tired on the phone.
I explained about the catapult.
I know You probably aren't excited about this idea.

Thanks for making Louise so happy.
Twelve pounds is a good start.
I'm going to go over during vacation
and work with her on exercises.
We can do them without the class a couple of
    times.

Jesus, surely You don't want to take Juan.
He's not that good a kid.
He could be if You'd give him time.
He's back in the hospital.
Louise and I lit two candles in front of Mary in
    church.
Please listen to our prayers, Jesus.

Thank You for Dad's promotion.
    He's really pleased.
He's talking about leasing
    a car.

Thanks for helping out Toby.
He's doing okay over the
    holidays,
except he didn't like his
    presents
and his brother is giving him
    a bad time.

Lord, Juan cannot be dying. You can stop the
    disease.
His folks need him. We all need him.
Make the drugs work. Surely You want him to
    live.
Mr. Freeman says the cancer has spread.
He says that all we can do is pray.
That's what we're all doing. Are You listening?
I bought the water balloons today.
We'll do the catapult the first day back.
Juan's mom held the phone for him
so I could tell him that.
I've been trying to read, but I can't concentrate.
All I can think of is Juan.
The Lord's will is mysterious.
Father C. would say that's too many words.
I guess it's all part of a plan You'll explain
    someday.

Bubba will bring a cellular phone to school
so we can give Juan a play-by-play report.
All we have to do is have a nurse or his mom hold
    the phone.
My hair's growing out already.
It seems just yesterday that we shaved our heads
so Juan would feel normal.

Louise thinks we're crazy.
She thinks I'll finally get kicked out.
It's good that she's gotten sure enough of herself

to tell me exactly what she thinks.
I had lunch with her, and she only ate one
    sandwich.
Thanks, Jesus, for helping her.
She's down almost twenty pounds now.

WB Day. I called the hospital and told Juan's mom
to be ready for an important phone call.
She sounded very discouraged.
She wasn't sure that he'd be able to understand.
We put everything out on the roof at lunch.
Please, Jesus, don't let the custodian
discover it before dismissal.
Everybody is so excited. All the guys are in on it.
Thanks for bringing us together.

We did it, Jesus.
And thanks for helping us escape.
Juan said, "Whoopee! Way to go, guys."
Bubba heard him on the phone.
The teachers, the safety patrol,
and the front-row kids all got soaked.
It was awesome!
Uh, oh. Brother just told Sis on
    the phone
that he wants to see me
    at 8:00 in the morning.
Be with me.

Well, I guess You wanted Juan bad.
You watched us crying at the morning assembly
after Mr. Freeman told us he'd died.
He had us join hands. That helped.
He said, "Together, with God's help,
we can face Juan's death.
He's in heaven because he was
    a good kid.
His spirit is still here with
    us in our memories of him.
It's good that he won't suffer anymore."
I know You forgive Juan for the kid tricks he
    pulled.
He never meant any harm.
Thanks for letting him hear about the water
    balloons
before he died.
Jesus, it'll be awfully hard for his folks.
Please help them.
A kid like Juan who's always into trouble
is really close to his folks
because they're always on his case.
He was a lot like me, Lord.
I know You'll find him a good place up there.
Now he'll know Father Coupal, won't he?
When Mr. Freeman announced it at assembly,
    I felt so bad.
I wanted to tell Juan that we'd have been good
    friends if he'd come back.
I hope he knows that.

Then I had to meet with Brother about the water
 balloons.
He knew the first person to ask, didn't he?
Thanks for getting me through that meeting.
Thanks for helping him understand
that Your paths are not always straight
and that one sorry, skinny kid is doing the best he
 can.

Louise

Well, God, it's late, but I wanted to write. When we buried Juan today, everyone was so sad. He looked so alive in the coffin, like he could jump up and say, "Fooled you!" Only he can't do that, can he? He's really gone. He's with You now, and we shouldn't keep crying about it, should we? But we can't seem to stop crying.

It's hard to think that heaven is a better place than here. At the funeral I felt more a part of the class than I ever have. Everybody hugged everyone else, and they included me. You know how it hurts when they leave me out, but at the funeral we were all feeling the same thing. The last candles Michael and I lighted for Juan are probably still burning in the church. The cancer went so fast. At least he didn't have to suffer long. I hope You're staying close to his family.

I stuck to my diet today. I used to think my family was fat because You gave us a fat gene, but now I think we're fat because we eat too much. You made Mom such a good cook, and we're all such pigs, eating everything in sight. Help me control my eating, God. Help my family control their eating.

That Jenny is so mean. When she said Michael had told her that I'd lost twenty pounds and she couldn't see that I'd lost anything, I wanted to slap her. She said it in front of everyone. And they laughed, of course. God, I know You said to turn the other cheek, but Jenny wasn't around then, was she?

Ben asked me for my social studies notes. It wasn't cheating to give them to him, was it? I meant to help, and he never takes notes he can read. He is so handsome, God. I wish he liked me. I mean, like he likes Jenny. I wish he'd call me on the phone and dance with me. I wish he'd take me to a movie. My folks wouldn't care. God, could You push Ben my way?

God, have You noticed how our car sags? It's been weighted down with my family. Our chairs all sag. The couch sags. We really need Your help. Neither Mom nor Daddy walks very well. All my grand-parents are dead, and I can see from the picture album that everybody was really fat. Please stop the fat from killing my family.

God, it's not fair. Mr. Freeman chose ten students who get to visit other schools for Catholic Schools Week, and he didn't choose me. You know how hard I work. You know how well I do. Bubba and Ben are going, and they never do anything. Jenny is going. All she does is giggle. If anyone asks any of those three kids questions, our school is going to be embarrassed.

It's because I'm fat, isn't it? He didn't choose me because I'm fat. God, can't You do something? I can maybe understand that the kids make fun of my weight, but a teacher is supposed to see the real me.

Who is the real me, God? Do You like me?

OK, God, I'm trying another personality. From now on I'll giggle at everything and I'll say "Boring" about anything new that might challenge me. I'll say "Like, you know" and "I mean" to start sentences. I'll be more Jenny than Jenny.

You heard me ask Michael if I should act differently. He's such a sweetie. He likes the old me, but no one else does. I want popularity. Is that so bad, to want to be liked? I'm not answering questions in class anymore, either. Lots of kids don't like people with the answers.

God, this doesn't seem like what I should write in a prayer journal. I meant to talk to You about good things, but everything else gets in the way. I offer You my efforts anyway. I offer You all the awful things that happen.

Thank You for my Kinder buddy, even if she did bring me a cookie today that I had to eat not to hurt her feelings. Why did Susan have to say, "I thought you weren't eating desserts, Louise?"

Dear God, I wish I were thinner. I wish I were bubbly. I wish Ben liked me. I wish I had blond hair. I wish I hadn't felt so stupid giggling all day. It's not going to work, is it? I'm still me.

Michael and I have exercise class tonight. Thank You for this one friend who cares enough to go with me. We're supposed to pick science projects this week. Help me to pick one that's not too hard. Girls aren't good in science, You know. Actually, You know I'm a science whiz, but help me do a project that gets me an A without making me look too smart.

Thank You for helping the coach see that I have potential. He says that if I go out for volleyball, I'll help the team with my serves. He says that since I've lost thirty pounds, I'm getting around the court better. The part I liked best was when he said that he was proud of me.

I've decided to walk to school from now on. It's only a mile. Michael suggested that I ride my bike. But You know how everybody would laugh about that. They'd think it was really dorky. Nobody rides a bike to school.

Lent begins next week. What should I do for Lent?

The Mardi Gras party is tonight. Thank You, God, for the beautiful dress. I know I look smaller in it.

Please bless the seeds I planted today and make my science project work. I want the marigolds that are fertilized to grow really well. I want different results in clay and loam. It seems pretty simple.

The kids are teasing little Fran. I remember how hard it was to be in the third grade and be so fat. Please help my little sister. Please dry her tears and make her little and popular.

Ash Wednesday. "Remember, Man, that thou art dust and to dust thou shalt return." I've been trying to think about what that means, God. I guess we're not supposed to think so much about what's happening here. But God, we are here. And seventh

grade takes all of my energy. I know it's not supposed to be important. Heaven and God are what's
important. But the things that fill my brain all day
are: What are the kids doing now? How can I fit in?
Have I lost weight today? I've decided to say the
rosary every day for Lent. I can do that in my room
at night, and no one will think I'm strange. God, I
want to be close to You. Please help me do that and
still be like the others.

Thank You, God, for all Your blessings today, especially for Jenny asking to study with me after volleyball practice for the science test. She'll walk home
with me, and her mother will pick her up after we
study. You know I don't have any girlfriends, no one
to tell secrets to. A girl needs that, God. Michael is a
good friend, but there are so many things I can't tell
Michael. I know Jenny is already close to Susan and
Kara, but she must like me, too, to want to study
with me. Now maybe we'll hang around together.
Maybe we'll go to the mall on Saturdays.

Thank You for Coach's praise in front of everybody. Thank You for my monster serves.

Dear God, why did it happen? Why did Jenny tell
everybody about my family? I was embarrassed and
hurt and mad. Really mad. I trusted her. I thought
she was my friend. And how did she thank me for
helping her with science? She said we were like
elephants! She said that in the hall in front of everybody. I think she even knew I was at my locker.
She's the meanest, rottenest person in the whole
world. If the bell hadn't rung right then, I don't
know what I'd have done.

Did she only come over so she would have things to laugh about? Do we really have mountains of food on our dinner table? Are we like elephants? Are my good, kind parents fools to be laughed at?

I've tried so hard, God, to be close to You, but where are You? I've said the rosary every night this week. Shouldn't I get some reward for that? No. I get Jenny. I'd like to climb into a box and hide for the rest of my life.

"Give us this day our daily bread." "I am the bread of life." Food and God go together, don't they? Only my family has gotten carried away. We love to eat. God, Jenny's right, we are freaks. We love one another, but it's not normal to eat like we do. I'm calling a family meeting tonight. Help them to understand what I'm going to say.

Well, God, they didn't like it, did they? But everyone's agreed, for Lent at least. We're going to eat less. No Sunday all-you-can-eat pizza after Mass, no dozen doughnuts for Daddy each day, no ice cream. One less of everything. Thank You for helping me show them that it's possible.

It is possible. I'm not hungry, and I eat half what I did. Their stomachs will shrink, right? It has to be a good thing.

We'll have our first game tomorrow. Please don't let me embarrass myself.

Thank You for my serves and for Coach, who believed in me. Thank You for Michael, who yelled himself hoarse.

One less of everything didn't seem to hurt anyone today. Daddy said he ate ten apples at the shop when he would have eaten doughnuts. Apples have to be better for him.

Why are four of my plants turning yellow? They have the best soil and plenty of fertilizer.

Rob says he has to stop eating less because he has to be big to play football in the fall. Please tell my brother that muscle, not fat, will get him on varsity. Fran says the teacher makes her sit cross-legged on the carpet to listen to stories. Please help the teacher see that it hurts Fran's fat legs to do that.

Everybody is so grumpy. Tuna fish is good for them, isn't it? Rob threatened to go to the pizza parlor without us when I told him that we'd have tuna for lunch after Sunday Mass. Please show him that losing weight is important.

God, I know jealousy is bad, but I can't help being jealous. Jenny and Susan drive me crazy prancing around in their cheerleader uniforms. Will I ever be thin enough to be a cheerleader?

Why are my plants dying?

What do You think of Michael and me quitting exercise class? He thinks I should sign up for ballet. Should I? But he says I have to go alone.

God, what have I done? I thought exercise would be good for them. Daddy only walked half a block, didn't he? I was so scared when they took him to the hospital. His face was white, and his hands were cold. He wouldn't have tried to walk if I hadn't pushed him. I should have left him alone. It's

It's all my fault. I can't change people. What if he dies? Dear God, don't let my father die.

I hate to see him lying there with all those tubes. The doctor wanted to admit Mom, too, when he saw her. Food is killing us, God. Please help us. I don't need to be a cheerleader. I don't need to be blond or pretty, and I don't care if a boy ever asks to take me anywhere, just please make Daddy better. Make his heart stronger. Send him back to his shoe shop, and I'll never bother You again with complaints.

Please don't let my family be mad when they find out that I talked to the clerk at the grocery store and changed our orders. With Daddy in the hospital, we don't need as much. We certainly don't need potato chips and whole milk. Thanks for the doctor who sat with me and talked about Daddy. He says it wasn't my fault that he had the heart attack. It was the fat.

God, are You watching over Mr. Freeman? He hasn't noticed the paper wads all over his wall clock. I wish he'd notice the cheating going on around here, too.

God, I'm down to two marigolds. How am I going to get an A on the project?

God, thank You for not taking my father. Thank You for sending him home next week. Thank You for showing all of them that we need to fight the fat. Thank You for the coach who talked to Rob.

I know I said I wouldn't bother You with unimportant requests, but please let the science teacher think I planned the death of the marigolds, that it all fits a scientific pattern of cause and effect. Thank You for the computer that made my report look so professional.

I hope You noticed how I helped Jenny with her prism project. That was a real sacrifice. You said to forgive, and I'm trying.

I love the ballet class. I know You weren't laughing at me.

We've made the tournament. Stay at our side, God. I love it when everybody runs to slap hands when we make a point. I love being a part of the team.

Daddy says he's lost weight in the hospital. Help us find a scale big enough to weigh him and Mom so they'll know they're making progress.

You've noticed that Rob is running every evening. I didn't think he could do it. Thank You for helping him.

Holy Week. Wash feet. Whose feet am I supposed to wash, Lord? What work do You have planned for me? I'm trying to get an education so I'll be ready. I'm trying to be a better person. I'm trying to be a smaller person. I promise one thing. I won't feed my family too much.

The stations of the cross done by the mimes were beautiful. They really came alive. I know You must love us very much to have gone through the Passion. I love the blessings of the fire and water. You bless everything in our world. I'll try to remember to look for You everywhere.

Daddy isn't very cheerful, God. It's wonderful to have him home, but he's not himself when he's sad. I can tell he's smaller when he slides down into his chair. It's easier for him to get around.

Thank You for my A on the science project and for having Miss Swensen notice my voice. I'm going to enjoy singing in the quartet.

God, we're only halfway through our social studies book, and Mr. Freeman is taking us out to play baseball every afternoon. I know everybody else is probably thanking You for that, but please whisper to Mr. Freeman that we still have a lot to learn.

Well, we didn't really expect to win, but thanks for getting us into the tournament.

Daddy went back to the shop today. Please keep him away from doughnuts, and let everything go okay. They say he has to lose another hundred pounds before they can do bypass surgery, and he has to be healthier. Please help him.

Thank You for my ballet class. I love to dance. I love leotards.

Mother says we're going to get new furniture, a new couch and living room chairs that don't sag. We're saving so much in groceries that we can buy the furniture on payments. I won't be ashamed to have friends over. I know I shouldn't ever have been ashamed, but after Jenny laughed at us, I couldn't bear to have anyone else over. Except Michael. Michael never laughed.

Why did the boys hide the new novels from Mrs. Garza? I will never understand boys.

Daddy has lost twenty pounds since he came home. That's not very much, considering how far he has to go, is it? I hope You're watching what he eats at the shop. Mom has lost thirty-five pounds. Yea!

I think I'm going to like the new girl, Gloria. She's quiet. I tried to help her around today. Jenny talked to her for a while, but she didn't stay with her or invite her to her lunch table. God, could I have one girlfriend all my own?

Cheerleader tryouts are in two weeks. God, I'm not skinny, but I'm not fat either. Could I be a cheerleader? I know I'm not bubbly, but I have a strong voice. They're going to pick twelve. I'll sign up tomorrow. Please don't let people laugh.

Gloria came over to talk about our novel. We sat in the porch swing a long time, talking. It's nice to have a girlfriend.

God, when I found Daddy eating in the kitchen, I didn't know what to do. It was the middle of the night. I woke up and wanted a drink of water. Then I saw the light. He stared at me like a cornered animal. Should I tell Mom? He says he won't sneak any more food. Please help him.

Mr. Freeman never got out of his chair today. We aren't learning anything. Now the paper wads are all over the duct work. Please help him be a better teacher.

Jenny and Susan offered to practice with me after school. Don't let them make fun of me.

I woke up four times to check the kitchen. Maybe we should put an alarm on the refrigerator. He'll die if he doesn't lose weight. Please help him.

I'm almost afraid to say it. Jenny was really nice
today. I think I can jump as high as any of them
can. I learned the tryout cheer. Please, God, help
me when I have to do it in front of everyone. Bubba said he thought it was great that I'm trying out.
Wasn't that nice? Michael says that trying out is
enough, that whether I make it or not, trying out is
a victory. He's afraid I'll be disappointed. Thank
You for my good friend. I won't be disappointed
either way. I've offered it all to You.

I think the doctor scared Daddy today. I hope it
lasts. Please keep him from food. Fran says she can
sit cross-legged now. Thanks for keeping her on the
diet.

I haven't been able to do any schoolwork today.
Please help me in tryouts tomorrow.

When I told Gloria about my family today, she
really listened. Thanks for my new friend.

Everybody cheered and clapped when I finished!
Thank You, God, for making me a cheerleader. I'll
be a really good one. I'll cheer for everyone, even
the poorest athletes. I know what it means to be
the worst, so I'll be there to cheer them on. I know
what it means to be down, and I pledge to perk up
everybody. I'll be bubbly.

But God, I'll still be me. Help me to follow Your
ways, and please remember to protect my family
from fat.

Lord, here I am, Jen, Jen, Jenny!
Your favorite cheerleader, at Your service.
Ha! Just *kidding!*
—Wasn't it great that fat Louise got cheerleader?
I mean really great!
You've done wonders with her this year.
I'm so glad, *really* glad,
because, You know, she's helped me a lot.
You made me beautiful,
but You didn't make me smart.
Thanks, Lord, for giving me Louise and Michael to
    help me.
I wouldn't even be a cheerleader if I didn't make
    my grades,
and I'd *never* make those grades without help.
I'm sorry for the times I cheated.
I haven't done it very much, not really.
Mostly I've worked and worked, and kids have
    helped me.
Bell's ringing—

Well, Lord, we're getting close to the end.
Like, school will be out in a month,
and then we'll have the long, *boring* summer.
Except that there's cheerleading camp and
    practice—
they're always fun!
—I suppose I'll have to go to Grandmother Nettle's
    for a week.
Lord, You know I *hate* to go there.
My real father will come over
and expect me to spend time with him.
You know I hate him!
I know You don't like hate,
but he's a *terrible* person.
He ran around on my mother and left her with me
    and Cheri.
Do You expect me to love him?
And Grandmother Nettle just sits and reads the
    newspaper.
She never does *anything.*
You can't want me to sit around there for a week!

Lord, this last novel is the *pits!*
I mean, really, it's *boring!*
It's about people in the 1800s
who aren't anything like us.
And they use funny words,
and the kids are so polite.
I mean, get real. *Nobody* is like that!
So why does Mrs. Garza make us read it?
—Lord, Mother and her husband are arguing a lot.

Please make them stop.
—Let's see, Lord, I've complained a lot.
There have been good things—
Thanks for the sunshine,
and the extra recess Mr. Freeman gave us.
—I thought those midgets were really funny,
waiting for the bus.
I mean, their legs were so short,
and they stood there holding grocery bags
just like they were ordinary people.
They didn't hear us giggling about them
when I brought the girls around to look, did they?
Louise said they'd be hurt if they heard us laugh.
—Do they feel things like I do, Lord?
Why did You make me beautiful
and them so *unbeautiful?*

Ce

Mr. Freeman is so *fun!*
He just laughed when we sprayed him with water
    guns.
Thanks for Mr. Freeman.
—I think Louise is going to be a *great* cheerleader.
Like, she really learns fast, and she's so graceful.
It's hard to believe she was ever gigantic.
—Lord, I've been trying to think
of what I could offer You, but it's hard.
Because everything I do is—oh, I don't know,
not very good, I guess.
I'm cheerful. That's something.
If You need a *smile,* here I am, Lord!

Oe

Lord, Cheri's been wearing my clothes again.
I'm sorry I yelled at her in front of her friends,
but nothing I have stays nice
because she's always wearing them.
And she plays on the playground in them,
and she *never* hangs anything up.
—I suppose I shouldn't have taken the shoes,
but they *are* my shoes!
I know it was hard for Mother
to leave her job to bring Cheri shoes.
I should have thought about Mother.
I'm sorry about that, Lord.
Don't You think I have some *rights* here?

Oe

I saw Juan's mother in the school office.
She was returning his books.
Somebody else will have them next year.
Did he write in them about what was happening
    to him?
That he was hurting or afraid?
He must have been afraid.
It's hard to believe that Juan started the school
    year with us.
When he set off the smoke bomb,
he was just a kid having fun.
Why did he have to die?
He was just an ordinary seventh grader.
You could snap Your fingers and take me, too.
Just *kidding,* Lord. No finger snapping!
Heaven would be all stirred up if I were there.
My mother *needs* me here.

—Her latest husband isn't working out, is he?
She is a really good person.
She's pretty, like me.
She works hard.
Why can't she find a man who's *faithful?*
Why don't You find her a man?
I know she was supposed to stay with my father.
—That's what the church says.
But he left us!
And he was a bum anyway!
Lord, we're supposed to trust You to make things
    right.
Mother and I are waiting, Lord.

Cee

I'm sorry, Lord, for that last entry.
I mean, it doesn't sound much like a prayer.
I try to be good and have good thoughts,
but then my head goes wandering off.
—Hey, where were You when the eighth-grade girls
    were smoking in the girls' bathroom?
Opening the windows to the playground was a
    good idea,
so the smoke went out instead of into the hall.
—Would You mind if I tried smoking?
Girls look so *cool* with cigarettes.
Of course, there's lung cancer.
I guess I won't try it.
—I don't see any prayer in this one either.
I meant to say something prayerlike.
—Thanks for Ben's note.

Qu

Lord, I'll be an *eighth grader* next year.
Then on to high school.
I want to be a cheerleader there, too.
And then what, Lord?
Like, I don't think I'm *smart* enough for college.
What am I supposed to do?
—I know I'm boy crazy.
You must have made me this way.
You made me so pretty that they all follow me.
But, Lord, I don't *want* to be like Mother.
I don't want a bunch of husbands.
I want one strong, faithful man.
I look at the boys in my class,
and I see problems with all of them.
Michael is always a step away from being
    expelled.
Ben cheats. They're all flaky.
Lord, I'm *scared.* I can't make it alone.

Qu

I'm *sorry.* I shouldn't have done it!
Like, Gloria is new and everything.
I shouldn't have put up the sign
asking for a date to the last party.
It seemed so *funny* at the time.
She hasn't had anything to do with the boys,
and to have her advertise for a date seemed
    priceless.
I had no idea she'd *cry.*
She was just like Louise.
She always used to cry,
and then we'd laugh.

67

We don't laugh at Louise anymore.
I'm *glad* Louise took the sign down.
I shouldn't have put it up.

Thanks for Mr. Freeman.
He knows we *hate* to stay in the classroom,
and he's taken us out almost every day this week.
—Mother's husband finally left last night.
Thanks for that, too!
I *never* liked him, You know.
I liked Tom, the husband she had when I was little.
He read to me and took me to the park.
He called me his little *pumpkin.*
What ever happened to him?

Hi, Lord, it's Jen, Jen, Jenny!
What a *fab day!!* No work!! Field Day!! Pizza!!
Thank You! Thank You!

Lord, please help me with the tests today.
These tests tell what we've learned this year, I
    guess.
—Like, they give me a headache.
I *hate* it when they send the results home.
Mother will sigh and say,
"You have to try harder next year."
I *try* as hard as I can, Lord. Help me.

Gloria was crying in the bathroom,
so I asked if she'd eat lunch with me,
and then we sat together and she was so happy.
I guess I should do that kind of thing more often,
    Lord.
Like, it's not that hard to be *nice.*
I really do know how.

Was it *bad,* Lord, that I wrote to Tom?
I just told him that he was my favorite father
and that Mother's last husband was gone.
—Ben says I can't dance with anyone else
but him at the last party.
That's a *laugh,* isn't it? Like, I'd stick with him all
    evening.
—Lord, I'm going to read this summer.
I've resolved. I'm going to read a book a week.
Can I *do* that?
Maybe if I do, next year will be easier.
Will a book a week make me a better reader?

One week left. Louise's father is in the hospital.
I told her I was sure he'd get better.
Please make that be true.
—Thanks for the yearbooks.
It is so fun to sign them.
Like, I found myself *fourteen times!!*

Everybody is writing such nice things.
—Mother had a phone call from Tom.
He's coming to see us!
Please, Lord, I hope he won't mention my letter.

There were twenty-six seventh graders who were
   smarter,
and Mr. Freeman picked *me* to help Mrs. Silver.
All of them would have done a good job,
but I was the one chosen. Thank You!
When I told Mrs. Silver
that I'd love to help her with summer school,
she was so nice.
They didn't have summer school
when I was a little kid.
Maybe if they had, school would be easier for me.
I'll make it *fun* for them, Lord.
I'll make them think summer school is the *greatest!*
I know how they feel,
worrying about passing all the time.
I'll be patient and do everything slowly,
so they can ask questions.
And I won't make them feel dumb.
That's important, Lord, not to feel *dumb*.
We'll laugh a lot at silly things, too!
They're little kids, Lord,
ten second and third graders.
That's when kids learn so much,
and if they get left behind,
they're like me, always in a *panic* about school,
always hiding that they don't understand.
I'll do my best, Lord, with Your help.

(signature)

Thanks for Tom.
Like, I know they aren't *married* anymore,
and some people would say he shouldn't be
    moving back in,
but I'm so *glad.* Mother is happier than I ever
    remember.
And they were married,
and marriage is supposed to last *forever.*
Tom listens to me, Lord.
I mean, he sits there and listens like You listen.
Please make it work out this time.
—When we told the eighth grade good-bye,
it was so sad.
They looked really *old,* dressed up like that.
We all hugged and cried and felt that everything
    was over.
They've always been there ahead of us, since
    Pre-K.
We've always wanted to be them.
Now we'll be the oldest for a year,
and then we'll scatter
to different high schools around the city,
and *nothing* will ever be the same.
We're so safe at Saint Ignatius, Lord.
Leaving here seems like jumping off a cliff.
Please help me be ready for next year.

(signature)

Hey, Lord, it's Jen, Jen, Jenny!
Your favorite cheerleader!
Just *kidding!* Just *kidding!*
This last day was a *riot!!*

Running through the hall with streamers was so
    fun!
I'm sorry if we left the janitor with a mess to clean
    up.
At least he'll have peace and quiet without us.
He can clean and mop to his heart's content.
—I'm not going to stop writing prayers
just because it's summer.
I know my prayers aren't very prayerful,
but I'm *trying,* Lord.
Like, I mean to be good,
and when I tell You what's happening
    and what I feel,
my head is clearer about things.
I stop to think about all I need to
    thank You for,
and I know You have truly
    blessed me,
even though I'm not *always*
    Your best disciple.
I'll need You with me while I
    work with the children this
        summer.
I'll need Your patience and love
    to share with them.
—Help me, Lord. I'm in Your hands!

Toby

Shifty-eyed, am I?
Well, Lord, I have to watch for the next attack,
    don't I?
They're all after me, You know.
Michael thinks You're the answer to everything.
He believes in You.
I think You're Santa Claus and the Easter Bunny.
I think they made You up to fool people into being
    good.
But they're not good, are they, God?
They lie and cheat and make fun of people.
And You made all of them,
so it's Your fault.
Michael's good, sometimes.
I like it when he listens to me.

Tommy says I stink.
Amanda won't sit next to me.

I got my uniform shirt out of the dirty clothes
    again.
Lord, why didn't You give me a mother who washes?
I'll bet Mary never sent You off in dirty clothes.
She probably made breakfast, too.
Michael says things can't be that bad.
I don't have cancer like Juan.
Shoot! Nobody'd notice if I did.
Miss Swensen says I have a nice voice.
Tommy says I sing like a girl.
I'm not singing anymore.

Brother caught me hiding in the stairwell, didn't
    he?
You probably tipped him off.
You talk to him all the time, I bet.
When he prays, You listen.
I'd been hiding for two periods, and no one noticed
    me gone.
Or maybe they noticed and were glad I was gone.
Brother didn't see the broken pencils I threw down
    the stairs.
I'll bet there's not a pencil in the fourth grade.
Good. They can use colors, fat, blobby colors.
They deserve to lose their pencils.
Will Brother call my folks?
They won't come anyway. They don't care.
Penance. This year's sacrament.
Did You see that I dug my pen
through the front cover of the book?
Mrs. Cather was so proud of our fancy penance
    books.
She thinks kids can reuse them for years

because we only need them for four weeks.
Guess I showed her, didn't I?
I'll get a different book every day and make holes,
    holes, holes.

Ha, ha. Michael asked me if I'm writing in my
    journal.
He thinks we're getting close, You and me.
But we're not close.
You don't care about me,
and I sure don't care about You.
I'm just writing for Michael.
I am telling You things no one else knows,
like I hate the whole fourth grade
and the teachers and the school and Brother.
I hate my own brother, too.
You know why.
He twisted my arm so bad this morning.
I still can't move it.
It's probably broken.
I watched You there,
hanging on the cross above the altar during Mass.
Your arms must have hurt.
But people cared about You.
They took You down and wrapped You up and
    cried over You.
Nobody'd cry over me.
They'd just leave me hanging.

Mrs. Cather says that my folks
haven't returned the parents' penance forms.

76

She's sent another letter.
You know it'll sit unopened on the dining room
    table.
They can see who it's from,
and they don't want to hear from the school.
Mrs. Cather says the rule is
that parents have to attend two classes
for the sacrament of reconciliation
before the kid can receive it.
Stupid rule. Stupid school.
She'll never see my parents there.
They'll sit behind their important business papers
during reconciliation,
and I'll be the only fourth-grade kid left out.
Left out again like always, huh, God?
Michael asked me to pray for Juan.
That guy is crazy if he thinks You answer my
    prayers.

Same clothes all week. Even I can smell me.
Michael says it's not all that hard to use the
    washing machine.
But why should I? I'm a kid. People should wash
    my clothes.
Lord, explain to me about the lady
with the cardboard picture hanging around her neck.
It looks like she used crayons to draw Jesus.
And there's His bloody Sacred Heart.
Is that what You're thinking of for me, Lord?
Am I supposed to get some cardboard and colors
    and string
and hang a picture around my neck?
That'd make me fit in, huh?

Why would You want anyone to do that?
Do You want us to think of You that way?
Didn't the lady hear the kids at Mass making fun
   of her?
Or does she only hear Your voice?
Okay, I'm going to try washing.
Help me, if You're not busy.

Clean clothes. Lord, didn't I get carried away?
The beds are clean. The towels. The smelly dish-
   cloth.
Ma laughed, and she made the beds.
Maybe You helped me, Lord.
Being good worked yesterday.
I'll see about today.
Vacation tomorrow.
Will they get me anything for Christmas that I
   want?
Please don't let the public school
junior high kids see me on the bus.
I know that if I cry they pick on me even worse,
but I can't help it.
Twenty-fourth penance book with holes in the
   cover.
You could stop me if You wanted.

Well, Christmas was another occasion at my
   house:
burned turkey, soggy mashed potatoes, everybody
   yelling,
and stupid books under that sorry tree.

My brother made me eat tinsel.
I'll probably die, and they'll cut me open
and find tinsel and send him to jail.
The jail part will be fine.
Michael's going to ask me if I've been writing.
So I'm writing.
He cares, Lord.
When the cardboard Jesus lady shook my hand
at Christmas Eve Mass, she wouldn't let go.
Why did she do that, Lord?
And she looked into my eyes
as if she could see all the way inside me.
I don't want anyone seeing inside me.
There's only tinsel and some other stuff there. Ha.
It's the other stuff that bothers me, Lord.
She didn't have her poster.
She looked like an ordinary old lady,
except for her spooky eyes.
Juan could hardly walk. He does need Your help.

What am I going to do about my book bag, Lord?
Mrs. Cather won't believe
that the junior high kids threw it out the bus
    window.
They hate us Saint Ignatius kids.
I don't know how come they hate me.
They think we have special privileges.
Yeah, uniforms and prayers.
Brother'll probably kick me out for losing the
    books,
and I'll be a public school kid.
I told Dad, and he said I should deal with it.
How am I supposed to deal with it?

Maybe if I get to school early,
I can swipe someone else's books from a locker.
Nah, teachers have the numbers written down.

Lord, Miss Swensen says I sing like an angel.
She says that I stood out during the Christmas
    program
and that my singing made all the difference in the
    fourth grade.
So what do You think of that, Lord?
Am I one of Your angels?
Brother called the junior high
and reported the boys who took my book bag.
They'll know I told.
How can I get back on that bus?
They'll be waiting for me.
I'll be thrown under the bus probably.
I'll be just a bloody spot in the road.
What am I going to do?
I could wait thirty minutes.
I'll ride the next bus and never see them again.
Did You help me think of that?
It was a good day. Amazing.

Too good to be true, wasn't it?
I got soaked by water balloons,
and I could hear Michael laughing.
I know his voice.
Saint Michael. Michael the good. My hero.
I hate him.
I hope Brother expels him.

I hope he has to go to public school.
I hope Brother gets them all.
I threw rocks at pigeons when I got home.
I bet I killed lots of them.
Your pigeons.

Lord, I didn't mean it when I said that they should
    be punished.
I didn't know Juan was one of them.
I didn't want anything bad to happen to him.
Remember, I asked You to help him.
I didn't mean for Juan to die.
Michael said the water balloons were for Juan,
a joke to make him feel like he was still part of
    things,
and not meant especially for me.
Surely You didn't listen to my stupid hopes.
What kind of God would listen to a kid like me?

I sang my best for the funeral.
I tried to make up for hating the guys
who threw the water balloons. It was so sad, Lord.
All of his family were there,
even his grandmother from Mexico.
I talked to Michael afterward.
He says I'm not to blame,
that You understand when I get mad.
Is he right?
Michael says he gets to stay at Saint Ignatius.
He isn't even suspended.
Brother understood about the water balloons,
    I guess.

We heard about the prodigal son today.
Mrs. Cather says You forgive just about anything.
I stopped the first-grade bullies from picking on
    Andrew.
He's a weird little kid, like me. Watch out for him,
    Lord.

Lord, don't You take care of Your own house?
How come you let Jules beat us up in the
    confessional?
We were supposed to be getting used to the room
so we wouldn't be scared.
Didn't You see him run into the reconciliation
    room
while Mrs. Cather was talking?
He punched me in the stomach. It hurt.
Tommy had a bloody nose.
We kept going in and staggering out,
until the cardboard Jesus lady stopped everything.
Maybe that's how You take care of Your house.
Maybe she's some kind of guard.
Jules sure beat it when she said, "Out, you
    naughty boy!"
Pretty interesting day. Mrs. Cather won't forget it.

Michael's been serving Mass, I hear.
I guess You don't want me to serve Mass.
I couldn't get there on the bus early, anyhow,
and my folks never know ahead

when they're going to be too tired for Sunday
   Mass.
That prodigal son stuff is pretty cool.
Did You like our prodigal son play?
Sure, I had to play a pig. What did You expect?
Mrs. Cather says she tried to call Ma, but couldn't
   reach her.
You haven't reached her lately either, I don't think.
I wish she'd go to the class.

So I'm getting good at washing.
Do You like me better clean?
I'm getting into this forgiveness stuff.
You'll forgive me as I forgive others.
When Amanda pushed my books off the desk on
   purpose
and I said, "I forgive you," I felt really free,
like I didn't have to do anything, not kick or yell.
Confused her, didn't it?
Now what did that get me forgiveness for?
Ruining the reconciliation books?
I'm sorry about that. I think penance is important.
And I want other kids to use those books.
A few holes won't stop them.

I like that feeling of forgiving.
I did my homework. Didn't have any plotting to
   do.
I forgive Ma for being a rotten mother.
I forgive Dad for living in outer space.
I forgive my brother for my broken bones

and all the mean things he's done to me.
I forgive You for forgetting about me.
I forgive the teachers for picking on me.
I forgive my classmates for everything.
Now You're forgiving me for all the things I've
    done, right?
Did I say I'm sorry about the pigeons?
You must be listening to me
or I wouldn't feel so good.

Lord, I still forgive, I do.
But Mrs. Cather says Ma only has one last chance
to take a make-up class,
and Ma says she doesn't have time
and that penance is an old-fashioned sacrament
    anyway.
Lord, I think it's a special sacrament for me.
One I need.

Well, there I was, hanging out, waiting for the bus,
when the cardboard Jesus lady dropped her
    groceries.
I think You put that hole in her sack.
Maybe You let those boys throw my books out the
    window
so I'd be waiting for the late bus.
Anyway, I jumped to catch her rolling apples
and I gathered up her cans, and she said I was a
    good boy.
A boy sent by God. Me!
I went into her house with her groceries,

and then she started lighting all those candles.
I saw the picture she copied the cardboard one
    from.
Funny, it wasn't scary.
It sounds scary, but it wasn't.
Did I need her for something, she asked.
"I need to have someone go to a class," I
    answered.
"Can I go?" she asked.
Just like that, Lord.
Her name is Mrs. Rodriguez,
and she's sure You won't mind if she takes Ma's
    place.
Adopted grandson, she called me.

Michael says it's a great idea
for Mrs. Rodriguez to take Ma's place.
My report card is A's and B's, and Dad is amazed.
He asked me if I wanted a beer to celebrate.
Lord, he doesn't have a clue about nine-year-olds.

When Mrs. Cather patted my shoulder
and told me I could do first penance,
I was so excited, Lord.
Only You could have sent Mrs. Rodriguez.
It's next week.
Now help me figure out how to get there at seven
    in the evening.
I forgive Jules for tearing up my spelling.
Forgive me for tripping him, even though he
    deserved it.

I forgive Ma for not washing.
I forgive Ma for not going to the class.
I'm sorry for anything I did wrong.

Lord, when did I start playing games at recess?
I just noticed that I'm like the other kids.
I was part of the team, and they were yelling for
    me to hit.
Thanks.

Michael's mom isn't feeling very well,
so I can't stay there and have them get me to first
    penance.
Jules doesn't want me to stay at his house and go
    with him.
What am I going to do, Lord?
Am I going to be left out again?

Well, Mrs. Rodriguez has come through.
I'll stay at her house overnight, and we can walk
    to church.
But Lord, I'm afraid of that house at night.
All those candles.
That creepy furniture.

My soul is clean as a baby's.
If something happens to me in this spooky house,
I'll go straight to heaven.

Thanks for forgiving all us fourth graders.
The penance service was neat.
Thanks for helping me walk beside Mrs. Rodriguez
   and her sign.
Thanks for Mrs. Cather and the parents at the
   reception,
who acted like Mrs. Rodriguez was normal.
Was I the only one who saw the cardboard picture
   of Christ
and His bleeding heart hanging around her neck?
Please help me get to sleep on this hard velvet
   couch.
Lord, thanks for everything, and help me to
   remember
You're always with me.
Help me not get so mad about stuff.
I'm blowing out the candle now.
Good night.

Ben

God, it's not fair.
I'll bet lots of kids didn't really read their books.
And old Mrs. Garza has to fail me.
And science too.
Who'd have thought that teacher would know
the crummy book I copied my project from?
I guess I should have changed some words.
Why can't they all be nice like Mr. Freeman?
Now I'll have to go to summer school with all the
    morons.
Oh, man, this is a rotten day.

God, Father, I'm supposed to think of You as a
    father.
Well, my father is a jerk.
He laughed when he heard that I have to go to
    summer school,
and he said I'd never amount to anything.

Is that right, God? Am I a loser?
Mom says I'm a late developer.
She says I'm her handsome, sweet boy
and everything will be fine.
She says Dad is just tired and he doesn't mean
    what he says.

You heard me talk to Brother Edward today.
He said that the grades will stand
and that I'll have to repeat seventh grade
unless I pass summer school.
His eyes never blink, Lord.
He didn't feel sorry for me at all.
I'm scared. I can't repeat seventh grade.
Everybody'd know I'm a dummy.
I'd be older than everyone else.
Help me, God.

Last day of school.
Oh, man, when I think things can't get worse,
something else happens.
I've never heard of a teacher
putting a report card in the wrong envelope,
but it happened today, didn't it?
I thought no one would know about summer
    school.
Then Michael brought me my report card.
When he said he'd read it before he realized it
    wasn't his,
I thought I'd explode.
Make him keep his word about not telling.

I shouldn't have threatened him.
"It's okay," he said, like I'd been nice or something.
God, why did You make me such a jerk?
I'm as bad as my father.
I'm sorry I make such a mess of everything.
I'll try to be better.

God, I woke up thinking about Juan.
He might have been going to summer school with
    me
if he'd lived.
He missed so much school.
He probably wouldn't have passed everything
    either.
We'd have had fun together,
making fun of the teachers
and throwing spit wads at the girls.
His folks were so torn up when he died.
Would Dad care if I died?
Mom would, of course. She'd be wasted.
But Dad would play the big man, wouldn't he?
He'd enjoy all the attention from his golf buddies.
And then he'd go on making million-dollar deals.
After all, he has my perfect brother Alex
to carry on his name.
I hope Juan is okay up there with You.
I miss him.

Lord, don't make me like my father.
When Jenny was flirting with those guys at the
    mall,

I went berserk. I shouldn't have grabbed her arm.
I left a red mark. I didn't mean to.
I love Jenny. I wouldn't hurt her.
I'm glad she stood up to me.
That's what Mom has to do to Dad.
She has to stop being so nice and making excuses
and stand up to him.
I won't ever touch a girl in anger again.
Please help me.

Summer school begins tomorrow.
I've heard it's easy.
Kids say it's just for dummies.
What if I fail that, too?
Please, God, let me be smart enough to pass.
Michael called tonight to wish me good luck.
You heard me thank him.
It's good to have a friend who cares.

Does Brother Edward know I'm ineligible
to play football for the first six weeks in the fall,
even if I pass summer school?
It's a dumb rule.
He's new. Does he have to know it?

Alex will be home tomorrow, too.
I've really missed him.
Bring him home safely.

Miss Fernandez is beautiful.
Thanks, God. She made the first day fun.
You saw me read everything as soon as I came
    home.

Help me do that every day.
I'm going to go over everything again before I go
    to bed.
Miss Fernandez says that your brain
works all night on whatever you read just before
    you go to sleep.
Mr. Powers was okay, too.
I like dissecting.

Lord, there's a problem with my lab partner, Fitz.
He needs a bath bad.
The formaldehyde smelled better than Fitz.
I know You love him, so I'll try to be nice,
but I'm going to need help.

Jenny wouldn't talk to me on the phone.
Would it be dumb to send her roses?
I guess I'd have to take them,
because I can only afford the ones
they sell on the street corner.
I'm really sorry I hurt her.
She doesn't have a new boyfriend, does she?

We're going to the airport to get Alex now.

Well, God, the second day was okay.
I guess You saw how I paid attention.
I didn't even look when paper airplanes sailed
    through science.

Alex went to Dad's office today,
and now they're buds.
At dinner Dad said, "It's nice to have a son to be
    proud of."
Yeah, instead of me, the loser.

Will I ever go to college and work in Dad's office?
It was fun when Alex shot baskets with me.
He said I shoot better than lots of high school guys.

Jenny wouldn't talk to me again.
I'll get the roses tomorrow.

Thanks, God, for keeping Fitz home today.
Laura sure smells better, and she's smart.
We aced our project today.
An A, God. Do You like me better with A's?
I guess that's a dumb thing to ask.
You don't judge people by grades, do You?
I worked hard today. I didn't cheat.
That'll earn me an A with You, won't it?

Jenny's mother took the roses.
She said Jenny would be pleased.
When I told her what happened, she frowned big
    time.
I wanted to tell so I couldn't deny it later.
Does that make sense, God?
It seems like telling about it will keep me from
    doing it again.
Why does Dad hit Mom?

Alex wants us to join a baseball team together.
There's a league forming in the park.
Thanks for my brother.
I promise not to let baseball get in the way of
    school.

Alex says he failed chemistry one semester in high
    school.
And he still got to the university, didn't he?
He says I'm smart enough. I just have to work.
Is that true, Lord?

I saw Jenny and Louise at the movies.
Jenny giggled when she thanked me for the roses,
    Lord.
Does it mean she's forgiven me?
They talked about cheerleading camp.
And Jenny's helping with the little kids' summer
    school.
She says summer school is a blast.
I wanted to say that I liked it, too.
But I couldn't.
God, I don't have to tell people, do I?

Hey, thanks for sending Fitz late
and giving me Laura for a partner again.
I went over and talked to him at the break.
He's not such a bad guy,
and I thought he'd need notes from the day he
    missed.
I'm trying really hard, God, to be nicer.

Oh, man, I was only driving the car out of the
    garage for Mom!
You know I've done it lots of times.
She was late, so I was helping her.
I thought it would be easier for her
if I pulled into the circle drive in front.
I didn't run over the lights on purpose.
God, the neighbors could hear Dad yelling a block
    away.

I'll pay for them out of my own money.
It's no big deal.
He didn't have to yell at Mom, did he?
It isn't her fault that I'm stupid.
God, it's awfully hard to love my father.
I don't know how my mother loves him.
Lord, I'm not going to tell You I'm sorry.
It was an accident.
But You could have guided me, couldn't You?
Maybe some good will come from it,
but I sure can't see what.

When Jenny invited me to go with her family to
    the beach,
I was so happy.
Then she said they'd leave Friday morning,
and I knew I couldn't miss summer school.
I felt awful.
I couldn't tell her the real reason.
I don't know what she thinks.
Lord, I've offered everything to You this summer.
I don't know why You'd want trouble,
but it's all I have today.

Dad posted the bill on the refrigerator for replacing
    the lights.
When I was a little kid,
Mom used to put my paint pictures on the
    refrigerator.

Tell Juan I miss him.
I'd like to call him up and toss a baseball with
    him.

Well, You saw my midterm report, all A's,
and Miss Fernandez wrote a note about my good
    attitude.
Thanks, God, for turning me around.
I couldn't have done it without Your help.
Dad's words hurt—"No standards."
But I can handle that.
I don't need to be a creep like him.
I know I deserved my grades.
Mom knows, too.

I think Miss Fernandez has something
in that reading stuff before I sleep.
I sure remember better than I used to.
But then, I guess I never went over anything
a second time, either.
Anyway, thanks.

The lights look okay, don't they?
Alex helped me with them.
Dad didn't even notice, did he?
I'm glad the stupid bill is off the refrigerator.

Laura asked me to a movie.
Cool, huh?
I guess girls can ask guys out if they want.
Her mother will drive us.
She's been a great lab partner,
and I'll miss her when summer school ends.
I never thought much about baseball until this
    summer,
but it's really fun with Alex.

He says that in high school
I can play football, basketball, and baseball.
He played them all.
And he bets I can get a scholarship in some sport.
But I need good grades, too.
He says he always had to work for his grades.
Thanks for a good day.

Almost everyone got sick when we dissected but
   me.
They were holding their stomachs and closing their
   eyes.
Not me.
That frog didn't bother me. It was already dead
   anyway,
and now I see how everything fits together.
Life is a miracle.
You created everything perfectly.
Mr. Powers said he'd never had a kid
who was so ready to dissect.
He asked if I'd considered studying medicine.
Me, Lord, dumb Ben. Wow!
And You know I was so interested.
I wanted to see and know everything.
That's why I checked out those anatomy books at
   the library.

When I called Michael
to tell him about wanting to study medicine,
it was kind of a test.
And, Lord, we both passed.

Michael didn't see anything wrong with my
   dream.
Thanks for helping people see that I'm not so
   dumb.

Laura and her Mom will be here soon.
I can't wait until I have time to start on my
   anatomy books.

Oh, man, I've offered You a lot of crummy days,
but yesterday was a new low.
All of those times when I was
jealous of Jenny talking with other guys,
I never thought of her caring about me with other
   girls.
Laura and I walked into that movie,
and there was Jenny.
When I introduced Laura, Jenny's mouth went all
   tight.
Maybe she thinks I didn't go to the beach with her
because I was with Laura.
And I can't tell her how I know Laura.
God, You were misunderstood, weren't You?

It got worse.
When I got home, Dad had my library books in
   the rec room,
where he and Mom were playing cards with the
   Andersons.
Dad asked me if I was doing research on girls.
I felt like a worm.
"We used to study *National Geographic*," Mr.
   Anderson said.
Mom just shook her head at me.

I said they were for school, but they laughed like it
    was a lie.
They think I'm a dumb pervert.
God, why is it so hard to be a kid?

Well, Jenny answered the phone at least.
I told her I had something to tell her.
Isn't it time I told her about summer school?
I'm tired of secrets.
Not telling about summer school seems like a kind
    of cheating.
God, I'm through cheating.
Help me face each day honestly.

Alex and I have had fun with our team,
even though we've lost more than we've won.
You can't win all the time, Alex says.
He's sure right about that, isn't he?

Lord, thanks for Mom.
When she said she wanted me to take back the
    library books,
and I told her why I had them, she believed me.
She said dreams are important.
Then she told me about her dream to open a toy
    shop.
Help her have the courage to do it,
even if Dad makes fun of her.

Wasn't Jenny nice? She didn't laugh.
She said she'd always been close to needing
    summer school.
And she said we both can have lots of friends like
    Laura,
but we can still be special friends.
God, she understood.
I even told her about wanting to be a doctor,
and she said I would be a good one.

Alex is packing for college.
Please stay at his side.
Since Juan died, I worry about people.
Keep Alex safe and bring him home again.

It's been a great summer.
I think that I've changed.
I know I can do things now.
Dad doesn't get to me like he used to.

I told Fitz and Laura good-bye.
We have one another's phone number.
I thanked my teachers.
When I said they'd helped me, I really meant it.

God, I'm going to work hard in eighth grade.
And whether I succeed or fail,
I know You'll be with me.
Help me to do my best with what You've given me.
And help me to know what's really important.
Dad's a mean man. I won't be like him.

And, God, Brother Edward doesn't know
about eligibility, does he?
So I guess, because I'm honest now, I'll tell him,
and then I'll work on getting good grades the first
six weeks.
After that, I'll be the star quarterback.
With Your help, of course. Later, Lord.

It's *me* again! Jen, Jen, Jenny! Live!
Well, Lord, I forgot to take my journal,
but I know You were there at Grandmother Nettle's.
Thanks for vowels and blanks in the Scrabble games.
Thanks for the talks we had.
It was fun to hear about the farm
when Grandma Nettle was growing up in Iowa.
I could just see her trying to get eggs
by poking corncobs at the chickens.

—My father tried to be nice, too,
even though I know he was a *rat* to my mother.
I guess I can't hate him
just because he can't love enough
and he only thinks of himself most of the time.
That doesn't sound like me, does it?
I *don't* think only of me, do I?
—I didn't like it when Cheri climbed into his lap.
Isn't she too big for that?
Or does she want a father so much that she
     pretends to be little?
—Summer school starts in the morning.
Guide me to help those little kids.

Ce

Jen, Jen, Jenny, reporting live!
It was so *fun,* Lord!
Those summer school kids think I'm *brilliant*
just because I can add and subtract.
And Lord, thanks for the *hunky* guy who moved in
     downstairs.
Cal, he called himself.
Like, he'll be a *senior* next fall, and he *talked* to me!
—Lord, take special care of Michael's mother
     today.
Michael's sure the baby will be a boy.
He already has Patricia, his older sister,
but a brother would be nice for him.
—Families are *important,* I know.
It'd be funny being an only child
with no one to kick under the dinner table.
You know I don't just kick Cheri.
She's always here to giggle with and share my
     space.

Thanks, God, for Cheri,
and I *promise* not to kick her too much.

Well, it rained, and we had to stay inside,
and the first graders all cried because of the
    thunder.
I mean it was *not* a good day, Lord.
Except that Cal waved to me as Mother drove me to
    school.

Please bless Michael's new brother, Stephen.
Help Michael not to care that his parents
won't name the baby Juan,
even though that's what Michael wanted.
—Is Juan throwing water balloons in heaven,
    Lord?
I'm being silly, I know. *Sorry.*
I can't imagine what heaven must be like.
It frightens me not to know, Lord.
—Thanks for how well I did with the children
    today.
Mrs. Silver said I was *wonderful.*

Lord, I don't know what to think.
I mean, I know my mother wouldn't like it
that I was down in the laundry room with Cal.
And I certainly wouldn't want Tom to know,

and have them arguing about me.
But Lord, I am thirteen and *very* mature for my
    age.
And You sent Cal, didn't you?
Seventeen isn't all that much older.
I thought he was going to *kiss* me
when he leaned against my legs while I sat on the
    washer.
Mrs. Mulligan really frowned
when she came in with her laundry basket.
I mean, really, she looked *shocked.*
Please don't let her tell Mother!!

Grounded!! No TV, even!
And all I have to read are Cheri's books.
Lord, I thought Mother went way overboard.
We only ducked into the bushes
because Mrs. Mulligan was watching us from the
    window.
Like, it was perfectly *innocent.*
Cal and I were telling knock-knock jokes.
—School was okay. Please keep that going for me,
    Lord.

What should I have done when Cal called?
I mean, You wouldn't want me to be rude.
And surely talking on the telephone can't hurt
    anyone.
His voice makes me tingle all over.
—Cheerleading practice starts tomorrow.
At least they'll let me out for that.

I hope we didn't make a mistake with Louise.
Lord, please don't let her get *fat* and make us look
ridiculous.

Q

Yea, Saint Ignatius!! We're the *best*!!
Our squad looks great!!
—When Louise's brother Rob drove up,
I couldn't *believe* the car.
Is it *safe* to drive it sagging like that?
I know he has to have an adult with him
because of the learner's permit,
but Louise's father makes the car lopsided.
Lord, You sure create some freaks.

Q

Cal says no one will know
if I pretend I'm going to bed early
and then climb out the fire escape.
You'd know, of course.
And Cheri would have to be ready to lie for me.
Lord, Mother and Tom are being *unfair* about Cal.
What did You think when Cal said he loved me?
Help! I need to know.

Q

I hope You liked our Math Monster play, Lord.
They have really learned a lot, haven't they?
And I hate to admit it,
but I didn't have my math facts down before this
summer.

—If You don't *want* me to leave Cal notes
in the philodendron in the lobby,
You'll have Mrs. Mulligan find them, right?
She's always here to do Your work.
Or she *says* she does Your work.
Lord, it must be hard for You to like
what people say is Your work.
But then, You know how everything fits together,
    I guess.
—Did You guide Mother and me
to that cute outfit for Michael's baby brother?
Coveralls, perfect! Can't wait to see that baby!

Cal says he'll write to me *every* day at cheerleading
    camp.
You haven't had lightning strike any of our letters
    yet.
Surely You approve of our love!
—I know You approve of Tom and Mother
    marrying again.
Like, they are so *happy* together!
Thanks for sending him back.
—Lord, I thought I was headed for *heaven*
when I followed Louise's father up those stairs and
    he tripped.
I could see his tons of fat rolling over me,
    smothering me.
Am I so bad, Lord, having thoughts like that?
Maybe it wouldn't be heaven I'd be headed for.
Just kidding!

Cal

Camp tomorrow!
I told my students good-bye this morning,
and they all hugged me.
I *love* hugs!!
—Cal *promises* he'll think of me all the time while
    I'm gone.
Someone watered the philodendron this morning,
but I could still read his letter.
I know I'm a fine one to talk,
but Cal is going to be a senior,
and he doesn't spell very well.
He says he's going to Harvard or Yale.
He hasn't decided.
I think You'd better help him spell.
—Thanks for finally sending him that delivery job.
He wanted to work, and no one would hire him
because his last boss didn't like him.
You should strike that guy with some *lightning!*
You should stop the things that are wrong—with
    lightning!
—What a blessing little Stephen is for Michael's
    family.
It was so fun to hold him, all soft and sweet
    smelling,
like a little construction worker in those coveralls.

Cal

Lord, *why* did Louise's brother Rob give me
a flower cookie when we loaded into the cars for
    camp?
I mean, I always talk to him,
and he's a great dancer for a large person,

but people might think he's my boyfriend,
and Cal might hear about it.
Why did I take the cookie and stand there like an
    idiot,
holding it by the stem while he took my picture?
Think of what could happen.
If we married, our children
might have my brains and Rob's fat!
Big and dumb!
And I'd have to love them anyway.
Like You love us anyway, no matter how fat or
    dumb we are.
Maybe they'd get Rob's brains and my beauty.
But I'm going to marry Cal
after he finishes at Harvard or Yale,
so I'll have to talk to Rob and tell him not to like
    me
because I'm spoken for.
Lord, please don't let him be too hurt.
—Camp is so *fun! Please* help my voice last!
No letter yet. Speed that mailman, please!

And I thought Susan was my *friend!*
What a lie! I know her sister isn't dating Cal.
She acted like she didn't even know about me and
    Cal, didn't she?
But You and I know she was trying to drive me
    crazy.
I was cool, wasn't I?
I never said that I even knew him.
He *loves* me. He's not *faithless* like Mother's
    husbands.

He wouldn't be seeing someone else, would he,
    Lord?
I mean, I know I'm only thirteen and Susan's sister
    is sixteen,
but I'm prettier.
Anybody would choose me over her, wouldn't
    they?
—Cheerleading is *exhausting*. One more day.

Well, all my whispered prayers worked, didn't
    they?
We're the *best*, and we have the *trophy* to prove it!!
Like, I've never hugged so many people in my life.
Thanks for our week and all the new friends.
—I'm really happy Louise and I were roommates.
I know I tried to get her switched for Susan,
but she was great to talk to in the dark late at
    night,
and she kept our room neat.
I know I'm a slob, but I like it neat.
And besides, Susan is a *liar*.
I couldn't bring myself to talk about Rob and Cal
    to Louise.
It wouldn't be fair to Rob to hear about Cal from
    anyone but me.
—I don't *understand* why Cal didn't write.
Maybe Mrs. Mulligan watered the plant,
and he couldn't read my address.
—It sounds wrong to pray just to get a trophy.
I mean that's how it sounds when I read it.
Lord, thanks for listening to me.

Oe

I don't understand the note from Cal.
He *missed* me, he said, and he lost the address,
and then it's all about *football practice* starting!
Lord, I know it's not true,
but I have to talk to him about what Susan said.
It can't be wrong to slip out for a few minutes
    tonight.
It's almost *life and death,* isn't it?
I'll wait until Cheri is asleep
so she won't have to lie for me.
—Mrs. Silver really covered a lot without me last
    week.
It felt good to be back with the children again.
I'm sorry it's the last week.
—When Mother said I'm not grounded anymore,
    I felt bad.
I guess that's my conscience talking to me.
If I don't listen to my conscience, what will
    happen?
Will it stop telling me when things are wrong?
Lord, I think I need to talk to Michael.
You aren't sending clear messages these days.

Oe

My face is still *burning with shame.*
How could Cal betray me like that?
He told the whole high school locker room
full of football players that I'm really *fast.*
A hot number, he called me!
You know that I loved him, and I thought he loved
    me.
And I only kissed him a couple of times.
Is that *fast,* Lord??

111

Now my reputation is *ruined!*
It probably was true about Susan's sister.
I don't care anymore, anyway.
And Rob is off the football team for hitting Cal.
You know how much he wanted to make varsity.
Why did You let him punch out Cal just for me?
As if I deserved it!
I should have *listened* to my conscience.

Lord, seeing Cal's black eye helps some.
Thanks for making me look out the
    window at just the right time.
Only I know You don't enjoy someone's
    trouble.
You had me look because I *needed* it.
It felt *good* to take Cal's note from
    the plant and *rip it up!*
He'll find the pieces all over the
    philodendron.
—Louise and I walked over to
    Michael's to play with
        Stephen.
Louise says that the coach
will let Rob try out for football
    anyway.
And she says that my flower cookie picture
is still tacked on Rob's wall.
I'm glad I didn't ruin things for Rob.
—Lord, Stephen is so *cute.*
When we all oohed and aahed over his smiles,
I thought about how little he had to do to make us
    love him.

He only has to be himself.
Are we like that to You, Lord?
If You can love me when I do so many *stupid*
  things,
if You look at me like I look at Stephen,
I know I'm going to be okay.
You love me as I am, cheerful, bumbling me.
I'm going to concentrate on eighth grade now,
  Lord.
I'm going to be kind and study and have *fun*
and *write in my journal always!*

again!

Louise again!

Food! We can't live without it, and yet it's poison for Daddy. Why don't You stop him from killing himself? Dr. Hastings said he gained four pounds this week. How can that be? Mom is serving good meals. He's cheating, isn't he? How can someone so kind and good do something so awful? Doesn't he know we need him?

It's hot, God. And Gloria wants to sketch all the time, outside. I don't have to go with her, but it's nice to have a friend who wants me around. We've about exhausted the park. She's drawn every child, dog, and bush, and I've read a dozen books waiting for her.

Gloria says she thinks Rob is cute. Wouldn't it be super if they fell in love and my best friend became my sister-in-law? It's funny, though. He disappears when Gloria is here. But when silly Jenny comes through the door, he's practically in the way. It's because she's beautiful and always flirting, but couldn't You help him look for more than that?

Are You taking care of the lady on the grocery store corner with the "Will work for food" sign? She was really sunburned today, and those pitiful little boys were so hot and sweaty.

Well, first cheerleading practice. I took notes on all the cheers and tried to keep up. They think it's great that I can do lifts. Poor, puny weaklings. That wasn't kind, I know. They can't help it that they're so skinny. Thank You for helping me fit in. Even Jenny was nice.

The lady the corner had a baby in a stroller today. I wonder where he's been other days. Are his diapers all he has to wear? I guess it's too hot to wear more. I'm going to take her a sack of canned food tomorrow. We certainly can give away some food.

Another good practice. Thanks for helping us work, even if it's over a hundred every day and we have to practice on the broiling parking lot. Why did the beggar tell me to go away? I suppose she's proud, but surely she took the sack of food I left. I didn't have any work to give her. Her sign says she'll work for food, so the food I gave her should make her happy. When I watched her from across the street, I saw her take money from several people. She smiled and thanked them. They didn't ask her to work for what they gave her. Does she simply want money? I hope someone was taking good care of her baby today, because only the two little boys were with her.

Gloria wants to draw the lady begging with her children. Is that cruel?

Only five days until cheerleading camp. Help us get ready.

Jenny says she has a secret friend. Why does it seem like her secrets always exclude me? I'll bet she told Susan and Kara, didn't she?

Michael's baby brother is darling. I want a baby like him someday, after I go to college and get a job, of course. And I want a nice husband like Daddy. Only please send me someone slim.

I hope You're listening to Our Lady about Daddy. I've kept a candle lighted in front of her statue in church ever since Dr. Hastings said Daddy's heart is a time bomb.

I was at practice, so I wasn't with Gloria when she sketched, but it sure looks like those are different children in her picture. Gloria is talented. She wouldn't draw girls for boys, would she? God, is there something wrong about the lady begging with the children? Are those children there to make people feel sorry for her?

Michael says it probably isn't against the law to use fake children. Well, they were real, but maybe not hers. God, what is my responsibility here?

"Beat it, kid!" she said. You'd think she'd like to have her children get away from that hot corner. I offered to take them to the school playground and the water fountain, and she was so rude. Maybe it was being responsible not to trust a stranger, me, but I only wanted to help. God, there were two

116

girls and a boy today, and none of them were the children I've seen before.

Weren't Gloria's sketches of the cheerleaders good? We looked just like ourselves.

The beggar liked the lemonade, didn't she? She actually smiled at me today. And those were the same little boys she used to have, and the same hot, fussy baby.

Why does Rob want to know exactly what time we're leaving for camp? Is he going to miss his little sister?

The beggar's eyes were black, weren't they? Somebody hit her. And all the children were fussy today. God, am I supposed to be doing something? I took her lemonade again, and I changed the baby. Was that enough?

Jenny burbled about summer school and how wonderful it is. God, how is it that whatever Jenny does is wonderful? No one in her right mind likes summer school, but according to Jenny, it's fun, fun, fun. Lord, I think I'm jealous. How can everything in her life be so right?

Michael is supposed to look after my lady on the corner. Do I have a God complex? Am I trying to fix things that You're taking care of? How are we supposed to know when You're giving us a job?

Well, anyway, I'll be off to cheerleading camp in a few minutes. Please let me fit in. Show me what the cheer is in cheerleading.

By the way, God, has Rob lost his mind? A cookie flower for Jenny. Ridiculous.

Back with the trophy, thanks. Thank You, too, for giving me Jenny for a roommate. She kept me focused on cheering, yet she made fun everywhere. I've never laughed so much.

Was Michael right that the man twisted the beggar lady's arm? Surely You want us to do something.

Please help Rob make varsity football, and don't let him overdo all that exercise in this heat.

Daddy's awfully pale today. Strengthen his heart, please.

The beggar finally let me take the children to the playground. Little Jimmy was so cute. I should have known I had trouble when the pickup rattled up and she ran toward us. That tattooed guy was so scary when he slapped her. I thought he was going to slap me, too. How could he hit those little kids? I sure see how she got the black eyes. Michael says we should call the cops.

That Jenny. Honestly! When I told her what happened in the locker room, she was totally surprised. How could she think a guy of seventeen would be in love with her? I thought she had Your special protection. Everything has always been perfect for her. Now everything's a mess, and she doesn't understand it. Poor Rob, her hero. He doesn't understand what happened either. He says she wasn't his girlfriend, so there wasn't anything wrong with her liking Cal. It's Cal he's mad at for lying about Jenny. He believes they were lies. Jenny says they were lies. Anyway, Rob's off the team for hitting Cal.

I wanted to smack Jenny. But she was sorry about Rob and worried that he was mad. So I told her the cookie picture was still up. That perked her up. She's never down for long.

Lord, what are we supposed to do about the beggar? "Please stay away from me," she said. "My husband will be back." Her husband. People sure mess up their life, don't they? Why did she only have the baby today? I lighted three candles, one for Rob, one for Daddy, and one for the beggar.

It was awfully hot when the ambulance came. The wheels of the stretcher left marks where they sank into the asphalt. Mother was so scared when she climbed into the ambulance beside Daddy. They left me with Fran. Neither one of us could stop crying. We're waiting now for Rob to come home. He can drive us to the hospital so we can be with Mother. Please let Daddy survive the surgery. He's young, not even forty. He lost some of the weight, didn't he? That was what they said he had to do. But another heart attack changes things, doesn't it? It can't be like Juan. Don't doctors know how to fix anything? He can't die. This page is all wet with tears.

Daddy's in intensive care. Please help him heal. I stayed home with Fran today. I'm trying to keep her mind off Daddy.

Michael checked on the beggar. Help us to convince the beggar that she needs the battered women's shelter. When the lady at the shelter told Michael that there was room, we thought it was Your sign that we should do something.

Daddy's still alive. Please hear our prayers.

No beggar today. Perhaps Your sign.

He's getting better! Daddy's over the worst, Dr. Hastings says. Thank You, God. Of course, surviving the surgery won't save him if he doesn't stop eating. Make him see that he's killing himself. Please help him care enough about us to stop eating.

Thank You for the coach's telephone call. Someone told him the truth about Cal. He's going to let Rob come back to practice.

Thank You for the taxi that pulled up just when we convinced the beggar to go to the shelter. She and her baby will be safe, and someone can set her broken arm. She'll need You to mend her spirit. Please make the child welfare people find a safe place for those children who were loaned out for begging. Neighbors' children, she said. What kind of neighborhood is that?

God, when I think of this past year, I realize how I needed You. Juan's death. My family's battle with food. Daddy's heart. My change from fat loner to me. I couldn't have faced it all alone. Eighth grade starts tomorrow. There'll be different problems, but You'll be there at my side. I'm counting on that.